TUNU AND THE BUCKETS OF STRENGTH

by

Sharon Jones, LMFT

A True Story

Alabaster Moments

ISBN: 979-8-9947095-4-2

Disclaimer: This book is intended for reflection and encouragement. It does not provide medical or mental health treatment and is not a replacement for professional care. For personal concerns, please consult a licensed healthcare or mental health provider.

For my father, Tunu, who carried heavy loads, worked the land and the mines, fixed what was broken, and taught us that kindness was strength.

This is a story about a boy named Tunu.
He lived long ago, but his love still lives today.

When Tunu was a little boy, he lived with his mother.
She was gentle, warm, and kind.

Tunu remembered how
his mother looked
in her candy-apple red dress.
Whenever he thought of her,
he saw that bright red color.

Tunu also lived with a stepfather
who was very mean.
He did not use kind words,
and he did not show love.

Every day, the stepfather made Tunu carry two heavy buckets of water, one in each hand.

The walk was long.
The buckets were heavy.
If even a little water spilled...

Tunu had to pour both buckets out and walk all the way back to begin again.

Sometimes Tunu wanted to cry. But instead, he took a deep breath and kept walking.

Inside Tunu's heart,
something was growing.
Not anger.
Not meanness.
But quiet strength.

When Tunu grew older, his mother became very sick.
She needed a new kidney, but help did not come in time.

Tunu lost his mother
when she was only 48 years old.
He carried his sadness carefully—
just like the buckets.

Later, Tunu lost his younger brother too. He was only 15. Tunu learned to be strong for others.

As a grown man,
Tunu worked very hard.
He worked in agriculture,
helping food grow from the earth.

Even after long days,
Tunu was thankful for honest work
and for providing for his family.

Tunu was very good with his hands.
He loved cars, engines, and machines,
and fixing what was broken.

When neighbors' lawnmowers broke,
they came to Tunu for help.
He fixed them so people would not
be charged too much.

Tunu believed helping others was the right thing to do. Fairness mattered to him.

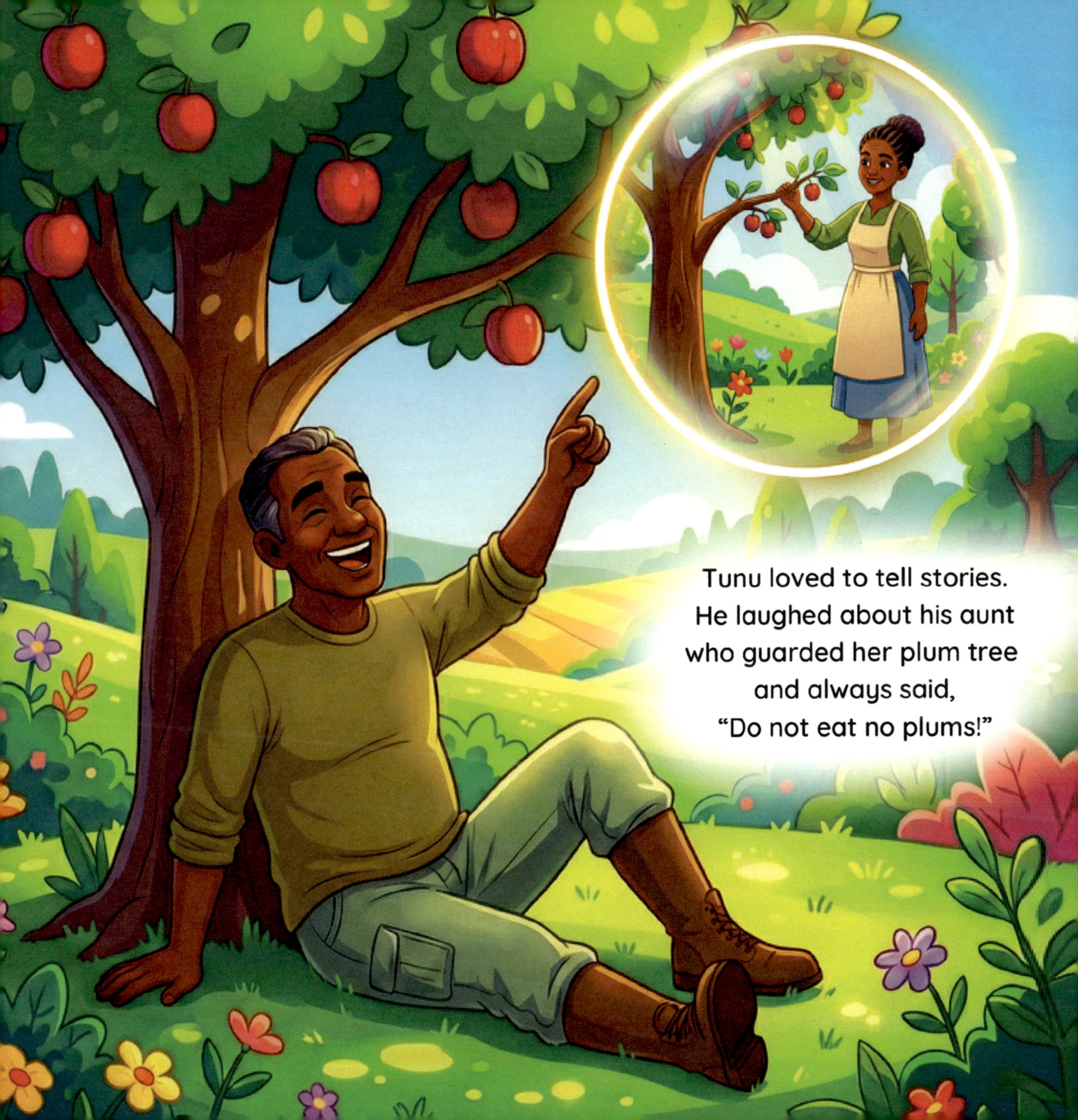

Tunu loved to tell stories.
He laughed about his aunt
who guarded her plum tree
and always said,
"Do not eat no plums!"

At mealtimes, Tunu always smiled and said, "Let the children eat first."

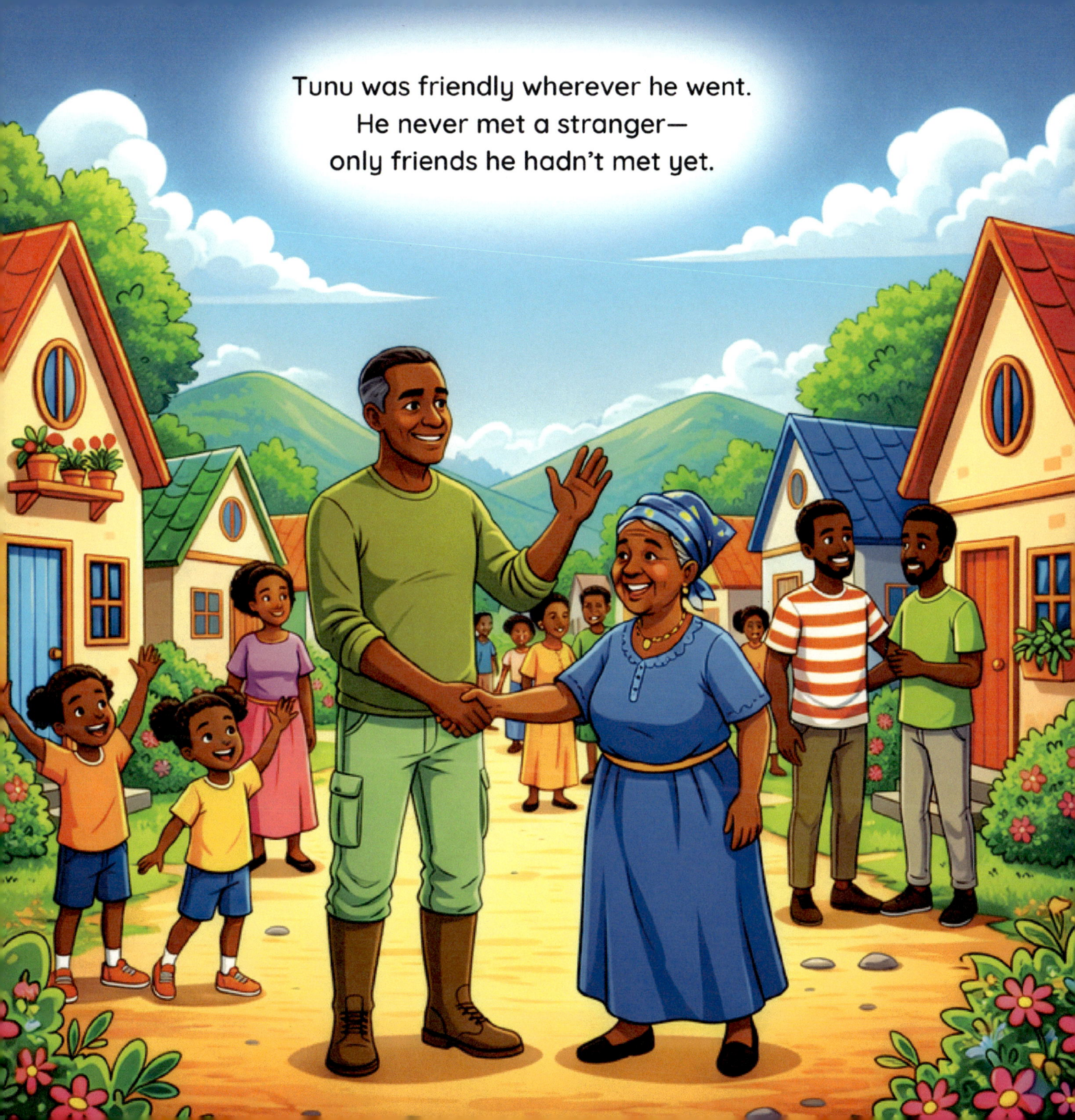

Tunu was friendly wherever he went.
He never met a stranger—
only friends he hadn't met yet.

One day, Tunu's journey on earth ended.
As his family laid him to rest,
the cows began to gallop across the land.

Some say it was nature.
Some say it was a sign.
But everyone felt it.
Whenever someone works hard with kindness,
protects others from harm,
remembers love in bright red dresses,
or carries strength gently—
Tunu is remembered.

Tunu is an African name meaning "one who carries and endures" and "a precious gift."
It reminds us of quiet strength, resilience, and love

"My father fixed lawnmowers to help people.
Sometimes all a mower needed was a small screw,
but he didn't want anyone to be taken advantage of."

Tunu and the Buckets of Strength is about the life
and story of a young boy who learns
that true strength is not loud or harsh;
it is steady, kind, and carried with care.
From long walks with heavy buckets to a life
shaped by loss, love, and honest work,
Tunu shows us that resilience can grow
quietly in the heart.
Inspired by a true story and rooted in
intergenerational wisdom,
this book honors compassion, fairness,
and the power of enduring with grace.

Let's Think and Talk!

What does being strong mean to you?

When have you pushed through something hard?

Who do you know that works hard and still shows love?

What helps you feel better when you are sad?

Can you be strong by staying calm? How?

Have you ever missed someone?

What did it feel like?

What would you say to someone you miss?

What happy memory makes you smile?

What makes your family special?

Who makes you feel safe?

What do you do when something feels unfair?

If you had a bucket of strength, what would you put in it?

About the Author

For more than three decades, Sharon has sat with people in their most vulnerable moments, listening to stories of loss, confusion, trauma, and a deep longing for change. As a Licensed Psychotherapist, she brings both clinical insight and a calm, comforting presence that helps others feel seen, heard, and honored.

Her writing and work with Alabaster Moments grew from a simple truth: even when life feels broken or overwhelming, we are not beyond repair. Like alabaster — soft enough to be reshaped, yet strong enough to hold what is precious — our hearts can be carefully renewed.

Through her books and reflections, Sharon hopes you will find language for your pain, courage to face it, and gentle guidance toward wholeness.

For more information please visit my website at:
healingjourneyalabasterusa.online

Made in the USA
Columbia, SC
06 April 2026